CFA Institute

AF731000

CFA INSTITUTE INDUSTRY GUIDES

THE TOBACCO INDUSTRY

by Ade Roberts, CFA

ISBN 978-0-938367-88-8
April 2014

ABOUT THE AUTHOR

Ade Roberts, CFA, is an equity analyst at City Financial Investment Company, a London-based independent investment manager. Previously, he was an investment director/portfolio manager at Analyst Investment Management Plc, a value-oriented fund manager in London. He is a member of the Education Advisory Committee of CFA Institute and the Structured Learning Committee of CFA Society of the UK. He holds the UK's Investment Management Certificate and has a BSc in mathematics and investment from London Metropolitan University.

CONTENTS

INDUSTRY OVERVIEW

The global tobacco industry generated aggregate revenues in excess of US$770 billion in 2012. The industry landscape in developed markets is noticeably different from that of emerging markets. In developed markets, industry volumes are in decline because of tax increases, tightening regulations, and demographic changes. Trading down is also prevalent in these markets because of limited growth in disposable incomes. In contrast, in emerging markets in Asia, the Middle East, and Africa, aggregate consumption is on the rise because of population growth and economic development. As their purchasing power grows, emerging market smokers trade up to midpriced and premium brands.

As **Figure 1** shows, the biggest single tobacco market is China, which accounts for more than a quarter of the industry's total revenues. In 2012, 5.8 trillion cigarettes were consumed globally, representing 0.2% growth over the previous year. Without China, global cigarette consumption would have fallen in 2012 by 1.7%. China's domestic market is controlled by a state-owned monopoly and is closed to foreign tobacco companies.

Figure 1: Tobacco Industry Retail Sales Value, 2012

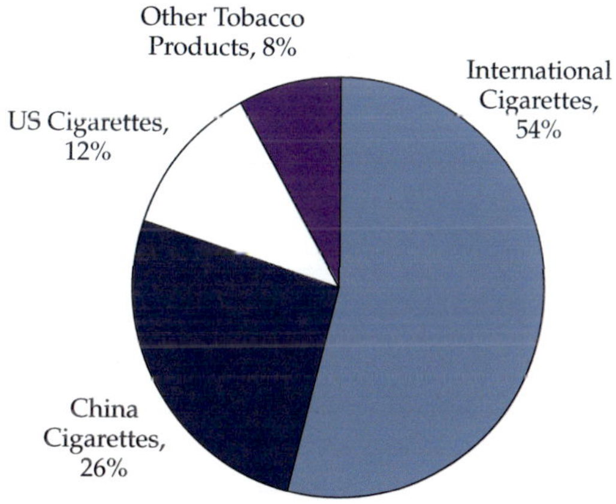

Source: Based on company data.

The next largest markets are Russia and the United States. Russia is unique in that foreign tobacco companies, as opposed to domestic players, supply more than 90% of the market. The United States remains one of the world's most profitable tobacco markets despite a long history of consumer and governmental litigation and tightening regulations.

Retail sales data are provided in **Figure 2**. Some 80% of the world's smokers live in low- and middle-income countries. Tobacco manufacturers have thus shifted their focus to these countries, which are not part of the Organisation for Economic Co-Operation and Development (OECD), where smoking is more socially acceptable than in developed countries and government regulation is limited.

Figure 2: International Cigarette Market, 2012

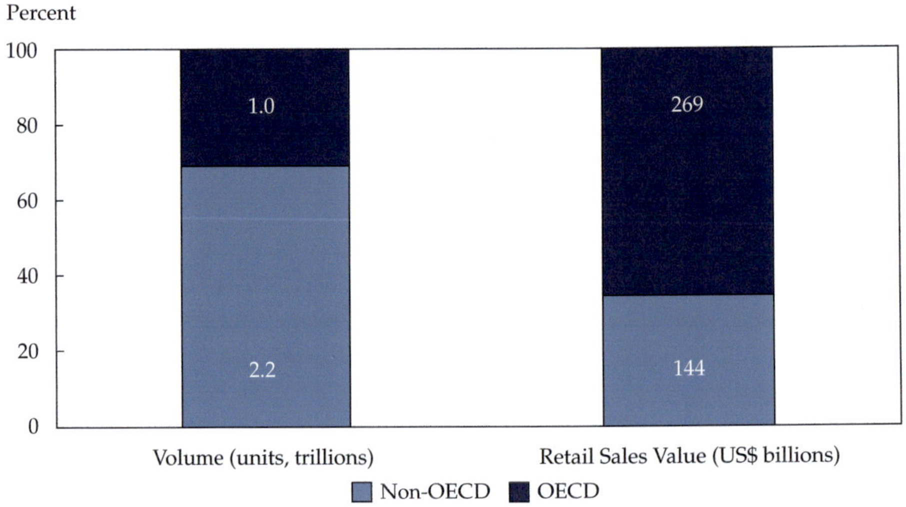

Source: Based on company data.

CIGARETTE CONSUMPTION: DEVELOPED VS. EMERGING MARKETS

Global cigarette consumption is driven by (1) the affordability of tobacco products, (2) government regulation, (3) social influences, (4) demographic trends, and (5) the marketing practices of tobacco companies.

In high-income countries, such as the United States, the United Kingdom, and Australia, tough regulation, increased taxation, and public awareness of the health risks of smoking have resulted in a structural decline in cigarette consumption. For every 10% tax-driven increase in the price of a pack of cigarettes in high-income countries, volume decreases, on average, by 4%. Half of this volume decline is the result of adults quitting smoking and young people not taking up smoking. The other half is the result of people who continue to smoke consuming fewer cigarettes.

Figure 3 shows the long-term trend in US cigarette consumption since 1900. From its peak in the 1970s, US per capita consumption has fallen by 72%. In 2012,

Figure 3: US Total per Capita Cigarette Consumption, 1900–2012

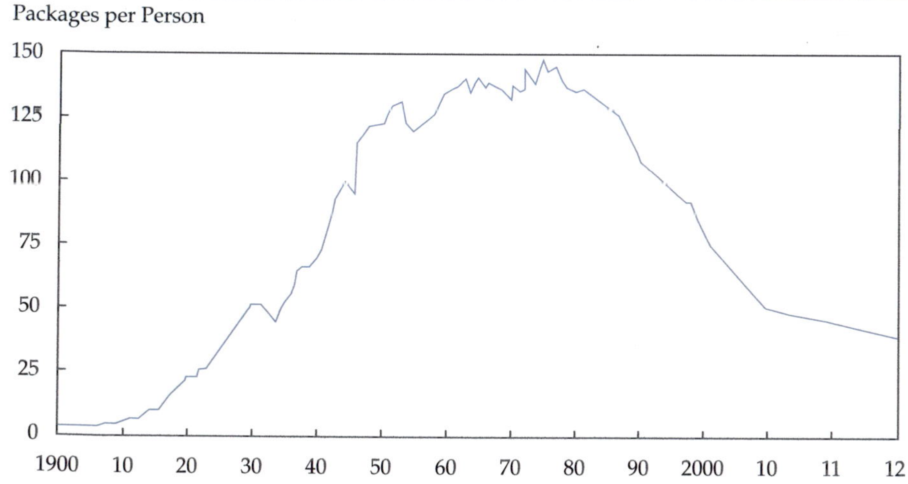

Note: A package is 20 cigarettes.

Source: Based on data from *The Tax Burden on Tobacco* (see Industry Resources section).

cigarette consumption per person in the United States was around 46 packages. This was the same level as in the 1920s, even though the US population has more than doubled since.

In contrast to this situation in high-income countries, per capita cigarette consumption has been growing in emerging markets. The reasons are (1) faster population growth, (2) increasing disposable incomes, and (3) less stringent regulation. The tobacco industry wields significant power in emerging markets because tobacco taxes may contribute up to 10% of a government's total revenue. As a result, there are few restrictions on tobacco advertising, which tends to reflect the aspirations of smokers to emulate users in high-income countries.

Figure 4 shows that in low- and middle-income developing countries, cigarettes became more affordable in the 2000s. The highest increase in affordability can be seen in China and Russia. (Affordability is defined as relative income price, which is the percentage of per capita GDP needed to purchase 100 packs of the cheapest cigarettes.) The top 20 cigarette markets by volume are shown in **Figure 5**.

OECD projections, shown in **Table 1**, indicate that by 2030, the percentage of the population considered "middle class" is expected to shift from Europe and North America to Asia Pacific in reflection of Asia Pacific's rise in living standards. This trend is expected to underpin demand for tobacco products in emerging markets.

Figure 4: Change in Regional Cigarette Affordability, 2000–10

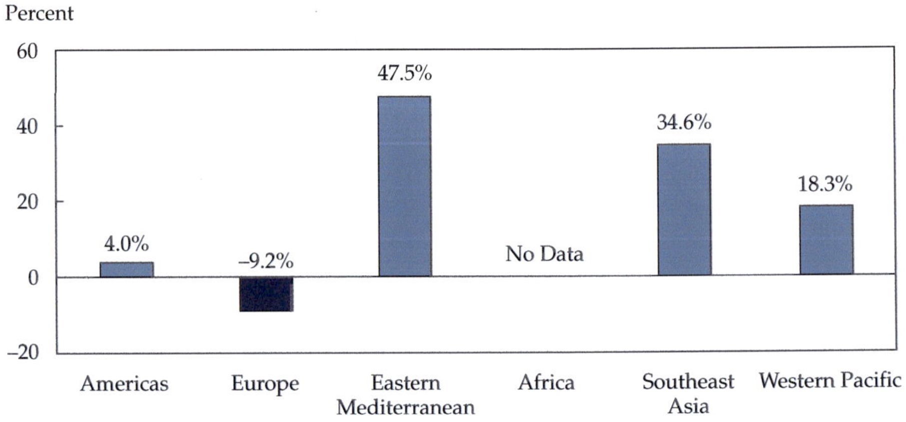

Source: Based on data from *The Tobacco Atlas*.

Figure 5: Top 20 Cigarette Markets by Unit Volume, 2012 (billions)

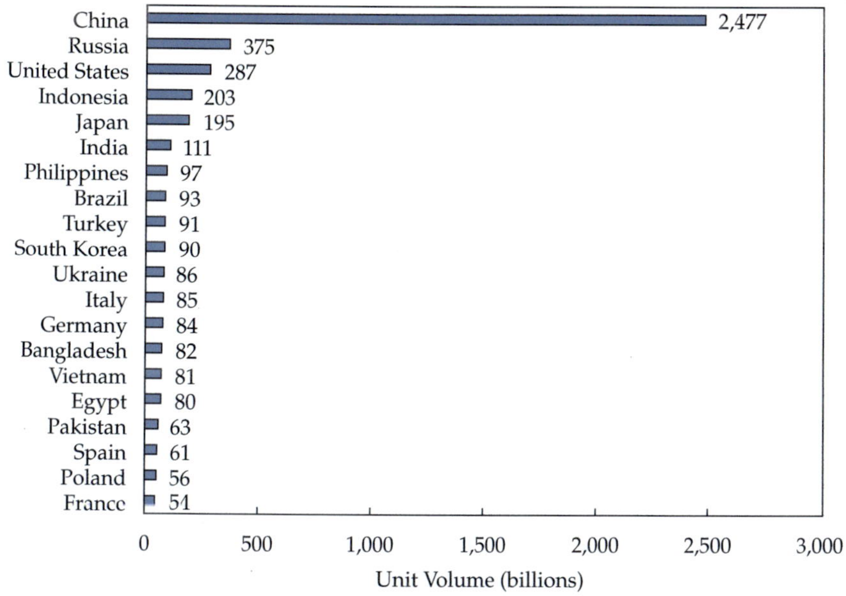

Source: Based on company reports.

Table 1: Global Middle-Class Population, 2009–2030E[a] (in millions)

	2009		2020		2030	
Region	Millions	Share	Millions	Share	Millions	Share
Europe	338	18%	333	10%	322	7%
North America	664	36	703	22	680	14
Central and South America	181	10	251	8	313	6
Asia Pacific	525	28	1,740	54	3,228	66
Sub-Saharan Africa	32	2	57	2	107	2
Middle East and North America	105	6	165	5	234	5
World	1,845	100%	3,249	100%	4,884	100%

Note: E[a] = Data for the final year are estimated.

Source: Based on data from the OECD.

OTHER TOBACCO PRODUCTS

As **Figure 6** shows, cigarettes account for 85% of the industry's retail sales value. Other tobacco products are available, however, that are cheaper or have lower health risks than cigarettes, including cigars and smokeless tobacco.

Figure 6: Tobacco Industry Product Categories, 2012

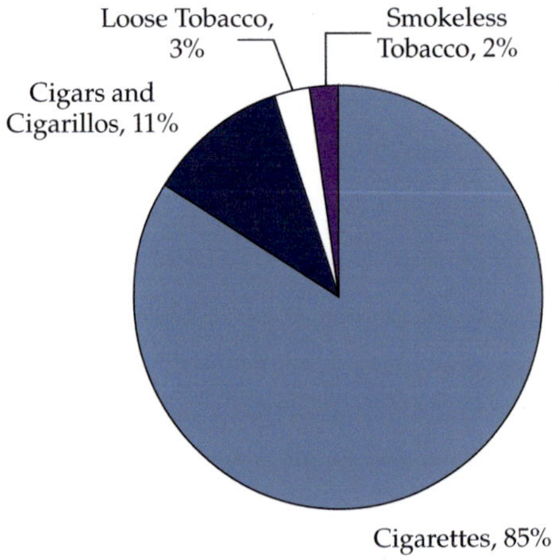

Source: Based on company reports.

CIGARS AND CIGARILLOS

Cigar consumption has boomed in the past decade in the key regions of North America and Western Europe and also in China. The reason is a perception that cigars are more stylish and less harmful than cigarettes because they are not meant to be inhaled. Cigarillos are smaller than regular cigars but larger than cigarettes and, like cigars, are wrapped in tobacco leaves or brown tobacco-based paper. Cigarillos exploit loopholes in existing legal definitions of cigarettes to avoid being regulated or taxed as cigarettes. This strategy makes them more affordable than cigarettes.

LOOSE TOBACCO

Also known as "fine-cut tobacco," this form is a cheaper alternative to cigarettes that is benefiting from cost-conscious smokers trading down in developed markets as higher taxation squeezes affordability. Loose tobacco can be hand-rolled (producing "roll-your-own" cigarettes) or sealed with a rolling kit (producing "make-your-own" cigarettes).

SMOKELESS TOBACCO

The most popular forms of smokeless tobacco are snuff, chewing tobacco, and Swedish-style snus (a moist powder that is placed under the upper lip for extended periods of time; it is pasteurized, is not fermented, and contains no added sugar). These products are viewed as less harmful than cigarettes and have benefited from smoking bans in public places in many developed countries. Smokeless tobacco is popular in the United States, India, and Sweden. Snus is banned in Australia and all EU member states except Sweden.

NEXT GENERATION PRODUCTS

The fastest growing segment of the industry, worth an estimated US$2.5 billion in 2013, is e-cigarettes, a type of which is shown in **Figure 7**. They are battery-powered

Figure 7: An Electronic Cigarette

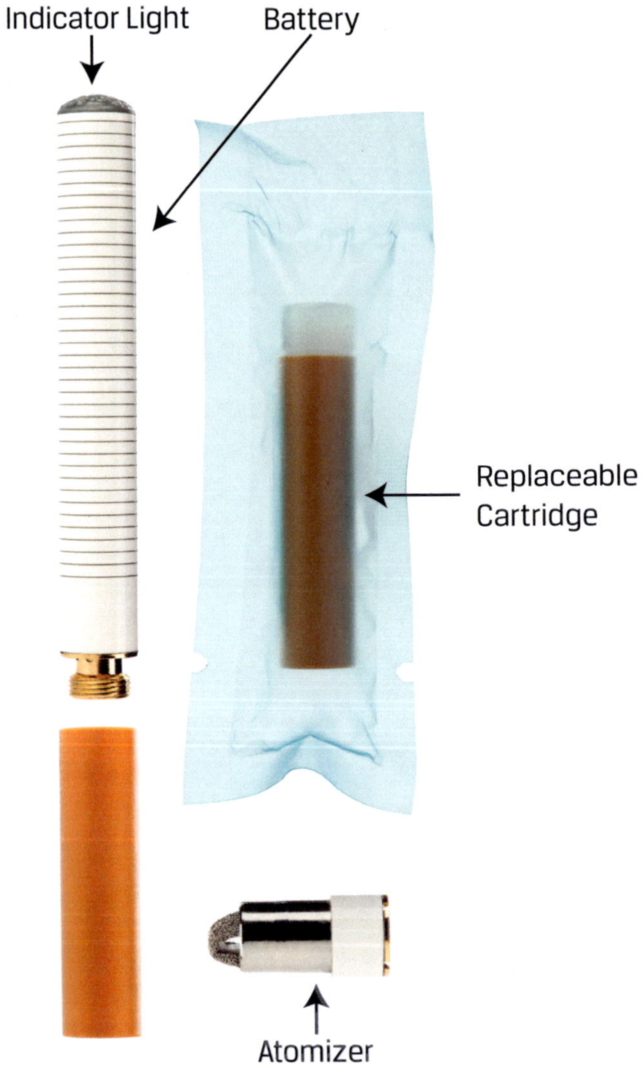

Source: ©iStock.com/Photo_HamsterMan.

devices with the look and feel of regular cigarettes. They simulate the act of smoking but contain no tobacco and produce no tobacco smoke, ash, or smell.

E-cigarettes were first introduced in China as an aid for smoking cessation and replacement. They are cheaper than regular cigarettes because they do not incur excise taxes. Although China continues to supply most e-cigarettes, domestic Chinese demand has failed to gain traction because regular tobacco taxes contribute 6% of official Chinese government revenue. **Figure 8** shows that domestic e-cigarette sales in China have more than halved since 2010. Over the same period, US sales of e-cigarettes have risen more than sixfold because of mass marketing and increased distribution.

Figure 8: Global E-Cigarette Sales, 2010–13E (US$ millions)

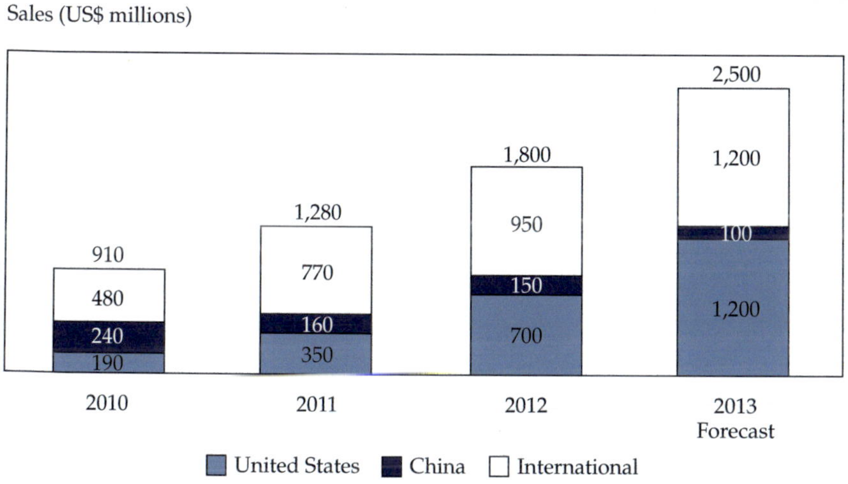

Source: Based on company reports.

Globally, more than 100 private firms, such as Apollo E-Cigs and Green Smoke, sell e-cigarettes. Most focus on only one or two markets. Incumbent cigarette manufacturers view e-cigarettes as a disruptive force that cannibalizes their existing products. As a result, they have been launching their own brands belatedly or acquiring start-up brands. For instance, in April 2012, Lorillard, the No. 3 US tobacco manufacturer, acquired Blu eCigs, the leading US e-cigarette brand, for US$135 million.

According to some estimates, the global market for e-cigarettes could increase fourfold, to US$10 billion, by 2017. At this stage, industry winners and losers are difficult to predict because of inconsistent regulation. Global regulations vary widely. Some countries, such as China and Russia, have no e-cigarette regulation, whereas others, such as Indonesia and Brazil, ban the product entirely. At issue is whether e-cigarettes should be classified as a medicinal product, a tobacco product, or a completely new category of consumer product.

LISTED TOBACCO COMPANIES

The universe of publicly listed tobacco companies can be split into three broad groups—global manufacturers, domestic and regional players, and subsidiaries of global manufacturers.

GLOBAL MANUFACTURERS

The four main players are Philip Morris International (PMI), British American Tobacco (BAT), Japan Tobacco International (JT), and Imperial Tobacco Group (IMT). Collectively, as **Figure 9** shows, the "Big Four" have a 38% global market share, which rises to 75%, as **Figure 10** shows, if China and the United States are excluded. By virtue of the size of its domestic market, China National Tobacco Corporation (CNTC) has by far the largest global market share.

- *Philip Morris International*. Formerly the international division of Altria Group, PMI was spun off in 2008 to protect the business from US litigation. PMI is legally based in the United States and is listed on the NYSE (New York Stock Exchange), but it has no operations in the United States. PMI operates in more than 180 countries and is the market leader in the EU, Turkey, Ukraine, Mexico, Indonesia, and the Philippines. PMI owns 7 of the world's top 15 international brands, including the non-US rights to Marlboro (the world's leading cigarette brand), L&M, Chesterfield, Virginia Slims, Philip Morris, and Parliament. PMI's local brands include Sampoerna (Indonesia), Fortune (Philippines), Optima (Russia), and Delicados (Mexico).

- *British American Tobacco*. A UK multinational company headquartered in London, BAT has since the 1990s evolved from a tobacco and financial services conglomerate into a focused global tobacco company. Some 75% of BAT's volume is distributed in emerging markets. BAT dominates Latin America, sub-Saharan Africa, Malaysia, Vietnam, and the Indian subcontinent. BAT's two major associates (i.e., equity-method investees) are the No. 2 player in the United States (Reynolds American) and the No. 1 player in India (ITC Limited). BAT's best-selling brands include Pall Mall, Kent, Lucky Strike, and Dunhill.

- *Japan Tobacco International*. JT is a former state-owned monopoly in which the Japanese government still maintains a 33% stake. Its international division was formed by the acquisitions of R.J. Reynolds Tobacco (1999) and UK-based Gallaher Group (2006). JT controls about 60% of its domestic market. Internationally, its main profit centers are Russia, the United Kingdom, and Western Europe. JT's major brands are Camel, Winston, Benson & Hedges, and Mevius/Mild Seven. JT also owns pharmaceutical and food businesses, but they contribute only 5% of group earnings before interest, taxes, depreciation, and amortization (EBITDA).

- *Imperial Tobacco Group*. IMT is the largest producer of cigars, fine-cut tobacco, and fine-cut papers. Since its IPO in 1996, IMT has been an aggressive acquirer of global tobacco assets and has risen from No. 2 in the United Kingdom and Ireland to No. 4 globally. The group's leading brands are Gauloises, West, Davidoff, and John Player Special (JPS). IMT divides its geographical footprint into "growth" and "return" markets. In growth markets, such as Eastern Europe, Asia, and the Middle East, its market shares are typically below 15%, so the group sees considerable scope for expansion. In return markets, such as the United Kingdom, Germany, and Australia, IMT's market shares are usually above 15%, and its objective is to maximize profit while actively managing market share.

Figure 9: Global Cigarette Market Shares by Retail Value, 2012

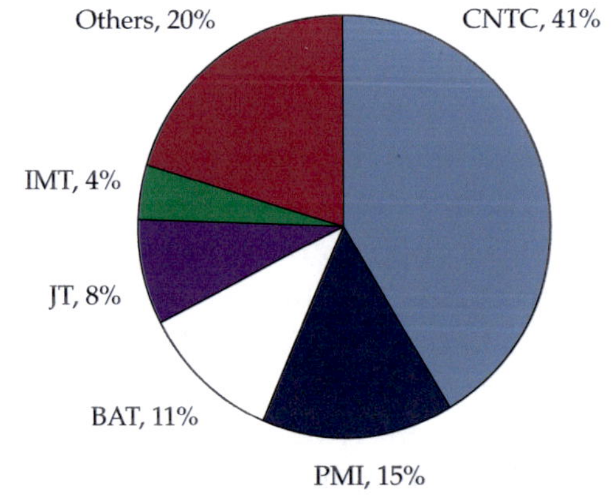

Source: Based on data from Euromonitor.

Figure 10: International (China and United States Excluded) Cigarette Market Shares by Retail Value, 2012

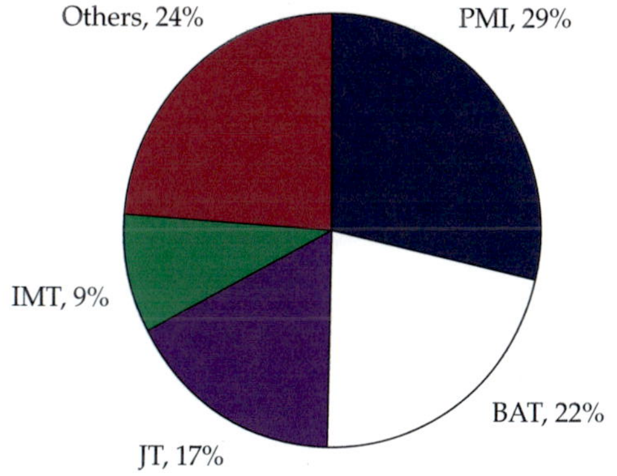

Source: Based on company reports.

The major brands of the global manufacturers are shown in **Figure 11**. Marlboro has been the world's No. 1 cigarette brand since 1972. In 2012, Marlboro's volume outside the United States was more than the combined total of the next two largest

Figure 11: Top Cigarette Brands by Volume, 2012 (billion units)

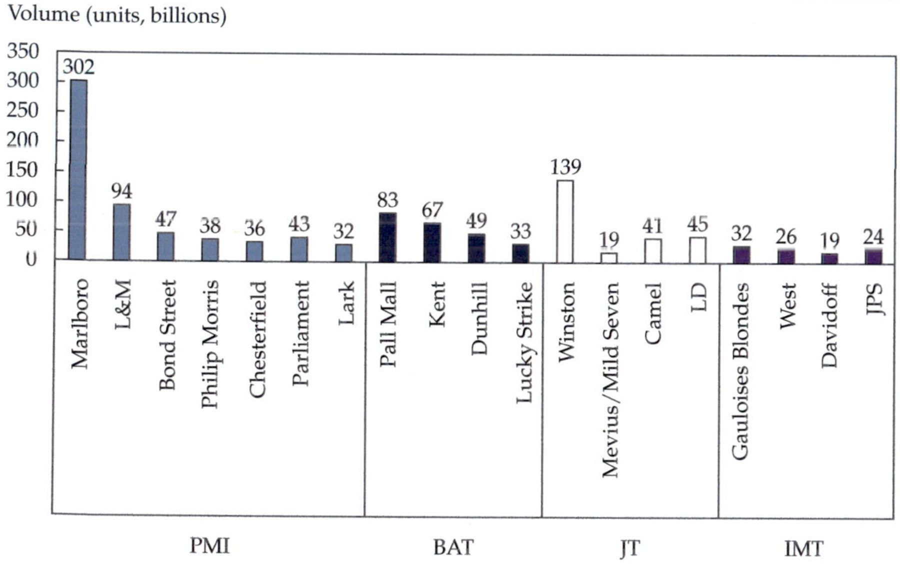

Sources: Based on company reports and author estimates.

brands (Winston and L&M). Over the past decade, the industry's volumes have been concentrated in fewer and international brands at the expense of many local and regional brands. This change reflects the trend of emerging market smokers to trade up from local to international brands.

DOMESTIC AND REGIONAL PLAYERS

These manufacturers have roots in one market and still make most of their profits from local brands in that market. They include Altria and Lorillard (United States), Korea Tobacco & Ginseng Corporation (or KT&G, South Korea), and PT Gudang Garam (Indonesia).

SUBSIDIARIES OF GLOBAL MANUFACTURERS

This group includes Reynolds American (United States), BAT (Malaysia), ITC Limited (India), and Souza Cruz (Brazil). These companies are listed on local stock exchanges but are partly or fully owned by the Big Four. They usually sell international brands in their domestic markets.

Table 2 shows the landscape of publicly listed tobacco companies. As the industry has consolidated into a handful of major players, fewer and fewer significant public assets have been left to acquire. The result is increasing cash returns to shareholders via dividends and share repurchases.

Table 2. Snapshot of Listed Tobacco Companies

	Ticker	Country	Market Cap ($ billions)	EV ($ billions)	P/E FY2014E	P/E FY2015E	EV/EBITDA FY2014E	EV/EBITDA FY2015E	P/FCF	Dividend Yield (%)	LTM Margin Gross	LTM Margin EBITDA	LTM Margin EBIT	LTM Margin Net Profit
Global manufacturers														
PMI	PM:US	US	134.9	159.8	15.6	15.5	10.9	11.2	16.5	4.5	26.2	18.2	17.0	11.3
BAT	BATS:LN	UK	98.8	115.7	14.5	14.0	11.3	11.3	17.9	4.4	78.5	40.3	35.6	27.4
JT	2914.JP	Japan	62.0	65.2	13.8	12.7	8.9	8.5	55.8	2.6	58.3	32.9	27.6	19.0
IMT	IMT:LN	UK	36.8	52.0	10.8	10.2	9.3	9.1	14.3	5.1	19.6	14.2	6.9	3.3
Domestic/regional players														
Altria	MO:US	US	75.2	85.9	15.7	14.6	11.1	10.7	16.3	5.1	42.4	33.8	32.7	20.9
Lorillard	LO:US	US	18.7	21.0	16.1	14.1	9.9	9.1	16.1	4.4	39.1	33.0	30.1	17.5
KT&G	033780:KS	S. Korea	9.4	8.6	11.7	11.4	7.5	7.3	34.6	4.3	56.0	30.6	26.0	15.5
Gudang Garam	GGRM:IJ	Indonesia	5.9	8.0	19.0	16.7	12.7	11.2	15.6	1.8	19.5	14.1	12.1	8.1
Swedish Match	SWMA:SS	Sweden	6.3	7.5	15.8	15.3	12.7	12.6	11.3	3.6	48.0	31.1	29.6	22.5
Ceylon Tobacco	CTC:SL	Sri Lanka	1.8	1.7	25.8	23.1	14.8	13.0	36.8	4.3	87.1	69.3	68.4	43.1
Vector	VRG:US	US	1.7	2.0	na	na	na	na	55.2	8.7	27.2	17.9	6.4	(0.8)
Universal Corp.	UVV:US	US	1.3	2.0	14.0	10.1	na	na	na	3.8	17.6	12.0	10.0	6.2
Huabao International	336:HK	Hong Kong	1.6	1.6	6.6	6.2	6.9	6.6	6.9	4.6	69.3	56.9	55.6	47.1
Karelia Tobacco	KARE:GA	Greece	0.7	0.4	11.8	na	4.4	na	18.4	4.4	78.3	9.2	8.5	6.4
Godfrey Phillips India	GP:IN	India	0.5	0.5	14.8	13.7	na	na	17.8	1.6	63.5	22.0	19.3	13.2
VST Industries Ltd	VST:IN	India	0.4	0.4	18.6	19.0	na	na	17.5	3.8	50.3	28.2	25.0	17.2
Alliance One International	AOI:US	US	0.2	1.6	7.0	4.0	9.1	8.8	36.0	na	11.2	7.6	3.7	(2.0)
Wismilak Inti Makmur Tbk	WIIM:IJ	Indonesia	0.1	0.1	11.4	10.2	6.8	6.1	na	0.5	28.2	13.4	12.1	8.6
Golden Tobacco	GTO:IN	India	0.03	0.03	na	na	na	na	na	na	32.3	(4.7)	(29.6)	(29.7)

(Continued)

Table 2. Snapshot of Listed Tobacco Companies (Continued)

	Ticker	Country	Market Cap ($ billions)	EV ($ billions)	P/E		EV/EBITDA		P/FCF	Dividend Yield (%)	LTM Margin			
					FY2014E	FY2015E	FY2014E	FY2015E			Gross	EBITDA	EBIT	Net Profit
Domestic/regional players														
Kothari Products	KTP:IN	India	0.03	0.03	na	na	na	na	na	6.1	38.3	30.7	27.5	25.7
Philippine Tobacco Flue-Curing & Redrying Corp.	TFC:PM	Philippines	0.02	0.02	na	na	na	na	27.1	2.2	57.5	41.9	29.9	19.2
Subsidiaries of multinationals														
ITC	ITC:IN	India	42.2	40.6	29.4	25.1	19.7	16.8	52.7	1.6	58.6	35.8	32.5	22.3
Reynolds American	RAI:US	US	26.6	30.2	15.3	14.3	9.4	9.1	22.6	5.1	53.7	36.7	33.2	18.9
Hanjaya Mandala Sampoerna	HMSP:IJ	Indonesia	23.4	23.5	na	na	na	na	42.3	3.5	26.6	19.0	18.6	13.8
Souza Cruz	CRUZ3:BZ	Brazil	14.5	14.4	19.7	17.8	12.5	11.8	17.8	4.7	65.5	45.3	41.5	28.3
BAT Malaysia	ROTH:MK	Malaysia	5.3	5.5	21.3	20.3	15.5	14.7	24.6	4.5	34.3	25.9	24.7	18.3
JT International Bhd	RJR:MK	Malaysia	0.5	0.5	13.2	na	na	na	30.5	3.4	87.0	12.8	11.8	8.5
Bentoel Internasional Investama	RMBA:IJ	Indonesia	0.3	0.6	na	na	na	na	na	na	16.3	(5.3)	(5.9)	(6.6)

Notes: FY = fiscal year. EV = enterprise value (the sum of all claims on the enterprise, debtholders, and equityholders). na = not available. P/FCF = price to free cash flow. LTM = last 12 months.

Sources: Based on data from Bloomberg and Thomson Reuters.

REGULATION

The degree of industry regulation varies around the world, but the global trend is toward more and more restrictive regulation. Typically, regulation that is successful in reducing tobacco consumption in developed markets is adopted in emerging markets within a decade.

FRAMEWORK CONVENTION ON TOBACCO CONTROL

Global tobacco regulation is primarily driven by the Framework Convention on Tobacco Control (FCTC) protocol created by the World Health Organization (WHO). The FCTC came into force in 2005 and provides the basic tools for countries to enact comprehensive tobacco control legislation. As of 31 December 2013, 177 countries accounting for 88% of the world's population had signed on to the FCTC. Ratification has yet to take place, however, in the important markets of the United States and Indonesia.

Signatories have six key objectives: (1) implementing price and tax measures to reduce demand for tobacco, (2) reducing environmental tobacco smoke, (3) regulating tobacco product disclosures and packaging, (4) banning or limiting tobacco advertising, promotion, and sponsorship, (5) restricting sales to minors, and (6) addressing illicit trade in tobacco products.

Although the FCTC is a coordinated effort managed by WHO, national governments have the responsibility to pass and enforce the legislations. To date, the FCTC's impact in emerging markets has been muted because the industry is a cash cow for those governments. The FCTC has fared better in developed markets, but its direct impact on consumption is difficult to isolate from the raft of other regulatory measures.

MARKETING BANS

More than 60% of countries have imposed some restriction on tobacco marketing. They include bans on advertising in national TV, radio, and print media. Partial restrictions have been ineffective in reducing smoking, however, because tobacco manufacturers have found creative ways, such as the internet and retail incentives, to redirect their marketing efforts.

Studies show that a comprehensive ban on all tobacco advertising, promotion, and sponsorship could decrease tobacco consumption by about 7%, independent of other regulatory measures. Some countries might experience a decline in consumption of up to 16%. Because tobacco remains an important source of revenue for many governments, however, only 24 countries, representing 10% of the world's population, have completely banned all forms of direct and indirect advertising.

Figure 12 summarizes the evolution of tobacco industry regulation.

Figure 12: Tobacco Industry Regulation

Source: Based on company reports and public data.

Product display bans. The implementation of product display bans varies by country, but the bans usually mandate that tobacco products be kept out of sight of customers—under the counter or in special cabinets. The bans are currently enforced in Australia, Canada, Finland, Ireland, New Zealand, Norway, and the United Kingdom.

Regulators believe that people are less inclined to smoke if they do not see the products. The impact on consumption has, so far, been limited, however, because tobacco is not an impulse purchase.

Public smoking bans. More than a billion people, or 16% of the world's population, are currently protected by comprehensive national smoke-free laws. Public smoking bans have been shown to prevent young people from becoming habitual smokers and reduced nonsmokers' exposure to secondhand smoke. In the United States, the smoking ban in New York City was credited with the reduction in adult smoking rates at nearly twice the rate as in the rest of the country. Also, a study of Massachusetts youths found that those in towns with smoking bans were 35% less likely to be habitual smokers.

Health warnings. Pictorial warnings, such as diseased lungs or bad gums, graphically depict the impact of smoking on a consumer's health. According to WHO, 30 countries, representing 14% of the world's population, meet the FCTC's best practices for pictorial warnings. The best practices include health warnings in the local language that cover at least half of the front and back of cigarette packs. Although the graphic warnings have high shock value, their impact on cigarette consumption is unclear.

Youth smoking prevention. Not-for-profit organizations, such as the Campaign for Tobacco-Free Kids and Action on Smoking and Health, have made significant progress in developed markets in banning all forms of youth marketing and advocating for price increases to make smoking expensive for young people. In the United States, "Kick Butts Day" is a national day of activism started in 1996 to promote youth awareness of the dangers of tobacco use.

Plain packaging. One of the nonbinding recommendations of the FCTC is for plain packaging. It would standardize cigarette packaging by removing all product advertising, including colors, logos, and brand imagery, and would enforce restrictions on font size and type. Regulators believe that plain packaging would reduce the attractiveness of smoking. This recommendation is potentially damaging to the tobacco industry because plain packaging makes it harder for manufacturers to differentiate their brands and for premium brands to maintain their price advantage over cheaper brands.

Australia was the first country to adopt plain packaging, which it did in November 2011. Ireland, the United Kingdom, and Canada are considering it. The tobacco industry is vigorously challenging plain packaging legislation on the grounds that the move would boost illicit trade and also that the confiscation of their brands would violate international treaties.

EU Tobacco Products Directive. The latest EU regulations will be implemented beginning in 2016. They build on the 2001 Tobacco Products Directive (TPD), which increased the size of compulsory labels on cigarette packs and allowed EU member states to introduce graphic warnings.

Highlights of the 2016 TPD are as follows:

- picture and text health warnings must cover 65% of both sides of cigarette packs;
- cigarettes may no longer be sold in packs of 10, which are more affordable to children;
- provisions to increase traceability of cigarettes will be strengthened to tackle smuggling; and
- slim and flavored cigarettes will be banned, except for menthol cigarettes (which reduce the throat irritation of smoking), which will be permitted until 2020.

TAXATION

Taxation is used to generate government revenue and to discourage tobacco use. According to WHO, a 10% price increase on a pack of cigarettes reduces demand by 2%–6% in high-income countries and by 2%–8% in low- and middle-income countries. Low incomes make young smokers more sensitive to price increases than adults.

Figure 13 provides a breakdown of the taxes levied.

Figure 13: Breakdown of the Price of a Cigarette (OECD Average)

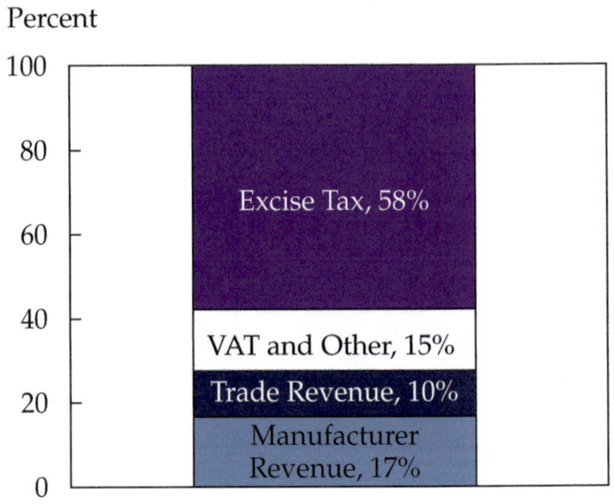

Source: Based on company data.

Governments typically levy three types of taxes on tobacco:

1. excise tax—a selective consumption tax often called a "sin tax,"
2. customs duties—a tax that applies to imported goods only, and/or
3. value-added tax (VAT) or general sales tax—a general consumption tax that applies to all goods and services.

Cigarette excise taxes are structured in various ways. Some countries, such as Australia, South Africa, and Norway, levy a *specific* tax, which is a monetary amount per cigarette. Other countries, such as Thailand, Paraguay, and Morocco, levy an *ad valorem* tax, which is calculated as a percentage of the retail price. These tax systems are known as "single-tier" systems because all cigarettes are subject to a single tax rate (either specific or ad valorem).

Mixed tax systems are also widespread. They combine specific and ad valorem components. All EU countries have mixed tax systems. Countries outside the EU with mixed tax systems include Switzerland, Russia, and Mexico. Many countries with ad valorem or mixed structures also apply a so-called minimum excise tax, which guarantees a minimum tax amount per cigarette irrespective of the tax structure adopted.

Other countries have even more complicated systems. Fairly common are multitiered systems that divide cigarettes into a number of categories (based on, for instance, retail price, the length of the cigarette, or the packaging type). A different tax rate applies to each category.

The various tax structures naturally result in large variations in cigarette price levels—both between countries and within them. In a specific tax system, for instance, all cigarettes in a country pay the same tax amount. In an ad valorem system, however, low-priced cigarettes pay less excise tax than premium-priced cigarettes. **Figure 14** shows the excise tax on low-priced cigarettes as a percentage of the excise tax paid by premium-priced cigarettes in several countries.

Figure 14: Excise Tax on Low-Priced Cigarettes as a Percent of Excise Tax on Premium-Priced Cigarettes, 2012

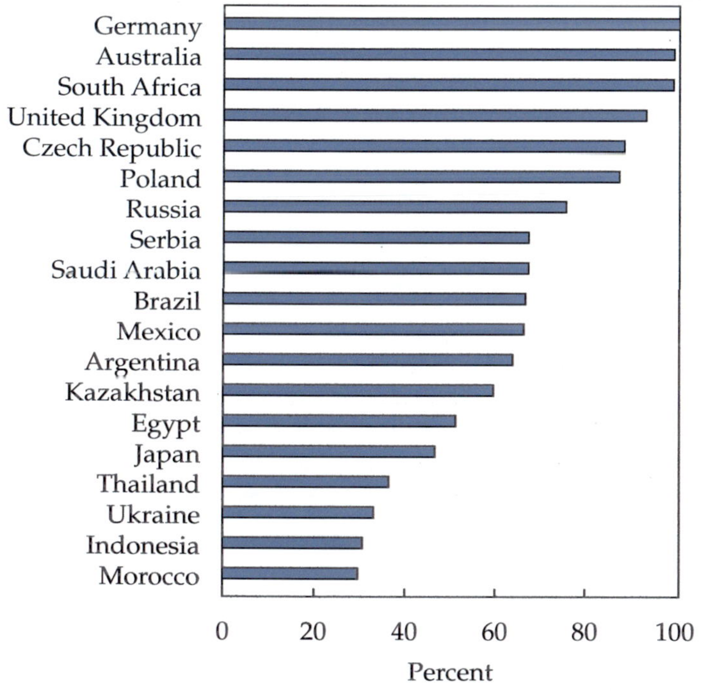

Source: Based on company data.

Other tobacco products in addition to cigarettes are subject to excise taxes in most countries. Many countries tax these other tobacco products at much lower levels, however, than manufactured cigarettes. **Figure 15** compares the tax level on Marlboro cigarettes with that on loose (fine-cut) tobacco for selected EU countries.

Figure 15: Total Tax Level on Marlboro vs. Loose Tobacco, 2012 (US$ per 20 cigarettes)

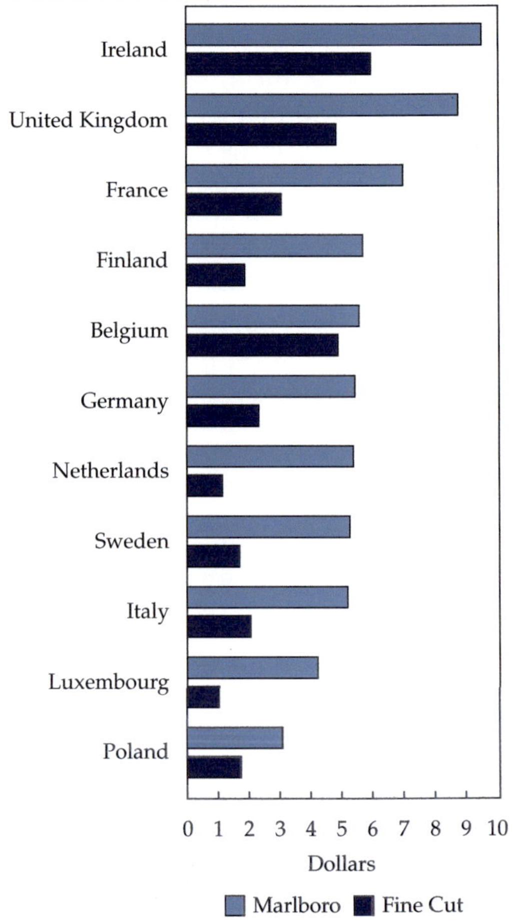

Source: Based on company data.

Figure 16 shows that tobacco accounts for less than 2% of tax revenues in developed markets, such as the United States, but up to 6%–9% in emerging economies. Many governments, therefore, have a vested interest in minimizing the social costs of smoking while maximizing the fiscal benefit of tax increases. Until new sources of government revenue are found to replace tobacco taxes, the industry is unlikely to disappear.

Figure 16: Tobacco Excise Tax Revenue as Percent of Total Tax Revenues for Selected Countries, 2012

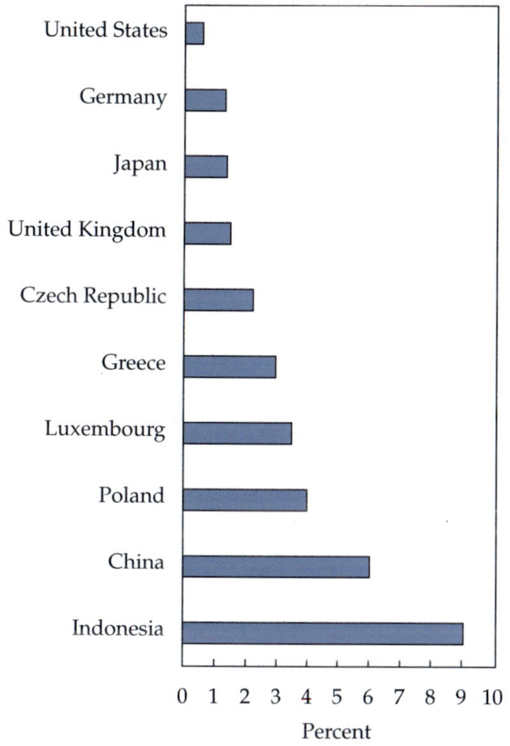

Source: Based on data from the OECD.

Unpredictable price increases encourage smokers to purchase smuggled or counterfeit tobacco, thus limiting tax and industry revenues. As a result, the tobacco industry advocates regular and coordinated excise increases rather than unpredictable movements.

Since 2000, the share of illicit cigarette trade in the global market has been relatively stable at 9%–11%. Illicit trade is greater than average in low-and middle-income countries. Illicit consumption thrives on the large regional variations in the retail prices of cigarettes. For example, cigarette prices range from US$12 per pack in Australasia to US$1.60 in the Middle East and Africa. Gray-market arbitrageurs have an incentive to export cigarettes from poorer countries to richer ones where their price is higher.

LITIGATION

Tobacco litigation originated in the United States because of the unique characteristics of its judicial system. For instance, the United States has a history of awarding high compensatory and punitive damages (awarded on top of compensatory damages as a deterrent or punishment), which motivates lawyers to work on a no-win, no-fee basis. The costs for a plaintiff of launching a case are, therefore, minimal.

Moreover, in the United States, each side pays its own costs. In almost every legal jurisdiction outside the United States, however, the unsuccessful party pays the winner's costs. Thus, outside the United States, potential plaintiffs face a large and real risk of substantial legal fees if they sue the industry and lose. In addition, potential damages are generally much smaller outside the United States. For example, punitive damages are unavailable.

Tobacco litigation usually revolves around one argument: whether it is the fault of the tobacco companies that smoking is harmful or whether this side effect is public record and is, therefore, the smoker's own responsibility.

The three main categories of claims against the industry are as follows:

1. *Recoupment actions*. In recoupment actions, also known as third-party reimbursement cases, health care providers seek to recover the cost of treating diseases linked to smoking. With the exception of the Master Settlement Agreement (described later), the industry has successfully defended most of these cases on the grounds of remoteness. Manufacturers have effectively argued that, even if an individual has a claim, the third-party plaintiff should not directly seek to recover any health care costs because that claim entirely derives from someone else's injury.
2. *Class actions*. In class actions, a group of people jointly bring a single claim alleging that certain common issues affect them all. Class actions originated in the United States and are still largely a US phenomenon. Plaintiffs seeking class certification must show common causation and must show that a class action is superior to other methods of adjudication.
3. *Individual actions.* These suits are brought by a single person alleging that he or she has suffered damage to his or her health because of smoking. The industry's tactic has been to fight these cases in every way possible, making the legal process slow and expensive for plaintiffs. In the past 50 years, plaintiffs have won fewer than 30 cases out of the 7,500 lawsuits filed in the United States.

LITIGATION HISTORY

The history of tobacco litigation can be broken into three waves.

1. *First Wave, 1950–1970*. When the first reports emerged linking smoking to lung cancer, plaintiffs used several legal theories in their claims:

    - Negligent manufacture: The manufacturers failed to act with reasonable care in making and marketing cigarettes.
    - Product liability: The manufacturers made and marketed a product that was unfit to use.
    - Negligent advertising: The manufacturers failed to warn consumers of the risks of smoking cigarettes.
    - Fraudulent representation of smoking's side effects.
    - Violation of state consumer protection statutes, most of which prohibit unfair and deceptive business practices.

    During this first wave, the US industry responded with full force, fighting each lawsuit and refusing to settle out of court. It relied on three arguments:

    - Smoking cannot be proven to have caused plaintiffs' individual injuries.
    - If smoking is dangerous, the manufacturers didn't know it when they made the cigarettes.
    - If plaintiffs changed brands over time, there was no proof a particular product had caused the plaintiff harm.

    The industry won all of these early lawsuits.

2. *Second Wave, 1980–1990*. In the landmark case of that period, *Cipollone v. Liggett Group,* the plaintiff and her family alleged that tobacco manufacturers knew but did not warn consumers that smoking caused lung cancer and that cigarettes were addictive. Although Rose Cipollone's husband was awarded US$400,000, an appellate court later reversed the decision. Other plaintiffs sued, claiming that tobacco companies knew cigarettes were addictive and caused cancer.

In defending themselves, the tobacco companies continued to deny a causal link between smoking and plaintiffs' illnesses. They argued that with the introduction of standardized health warnings and publicity about the claimed dangers of smoking, Rose Cipollone and other plaintiffs had knowingly assumed the risks of cancer and other health problems when they began or continued smoking.

For the most part, the tobacco companies were successful in these lawsuits.

3. *Third Wave, 1998–2003*. In 1998, six million confidential industry documents became available to the public as a result of legal action. The documents provided damning evidence that industry executives knew about the dangers of smoking. Plaintiffs now argued that the industry had covered up the reality of the effects of smoking at a time when the general public was unaware of this danger. These actions suggested negligence, fraud, and intentional misrepresentation on the industry's part.

   The first big win for plaintiffs occurred in February 2000, when a California jury ordered Philip Morris to pay US$51.5 million to a California smoker with inoperable lung cancer. Around this time, more than 40 US states also sued the industry under state protection and antitrust laws. The states argued that cigarettes contribute to health problems that had triggered significant costs for public health systems.

   In November 1998, the attorneys general of 46 US states and the four largest US tobacco companies (Philip Morris, R.J. Reynolds, Brown & Williamson, and Lorillard) agreed to settle the state cases. Terms of the settlement are referred to as the "Master Settlement Agreement" (MSA). The highlights are as follows:

   - Tobacco companies agreed to pay US$10 billion annually to the 46 states to compensate them for health care costs related to smoking. This amount equates to a minimum of US$206 billion over the first 25 years.

   - Tobacco manufacturers agreed to refrain from engaging in certain advertising practices, particularly ad campaigns that marketed cigarettes to children.

   - Tobacco companies dissolved three of their biggest industry bodies, the Tobacco Institute, the Center for Indoor Air Research, and the Council for Tobacco Research.

Attempts to pass on the annual US$10 billion costs of the settlement to consumers led to significant volume declines for the US industry and enabled new entrants, those unencumbered by the MSA, to undercut the established players. In late 2002, branded manufacturers were forced to lower their prices to regain market share from generic rivals. Between 1998 and 2003, US volumes fell by 20%; industry profits for the branded players were down by around 30%. Industry profitability did not reach 2001 levels again until 2006.

2003 TO THE PRESENT

In recent years, the US industry has had a mixed record in litigation. This result reflects the growing influence of the anti-tobacco lobby, which has become a potent political force in US state legislatures. Some examples of litigation follow:

- *Engle Progeny*. In 2006, the Florida Supreme Court dismissed a class-action lawsuit brought on behalf of 700,000 smokers and their families against the industry. In its ruling, the court found that the industry knowingly sold harmful products and kept the health risks of smoking concealed. The case could not proceed as a class action, however, because the court ruled that each case had to be proven individually. The ruling paved the way for more than 8,000 smokers and their families to bring individual lawsuits against the industry. These cases are ongoing.

- *Light cigarettes*. Plaintiffs in these cases alleged that tobacco companies advertise light cigarettes as healthier than regular cigarettes, when, in fact, light cigarettes merely use a special filter to dilute the smoke inhaled by smokers and are no healthier than regular cigarettes. The industry's response was that "light" refers to the taste of the cigarettes, not the amount of nicotine ingested, and that consumers should understand what the word "light" means. Also, raising federal preemption as a defense against state class-action lawsuits, the industry argued that US federal legislation regarding cigarette advertising supersedes state laws that prohibit deceptive advertising practices. In 2008, the US Supreme Court threw out the industry's preemption argument in a class-action light cigarette lawsuit brought in Maine. In allowing the Maine case to proceed, the Supreme Court ruled that federal legislation does not preempt plaintiffs from suing under certain state unfair business practice laws.

Meanwhile, since 2004, equity investors have warmed to US tobacco stocks in response to favorable rulings in major cases that have reduced the likelihood of the industry going bankrupt. In 2002, the California Supreme Court ruled (in *Myers v. Philip Morris*) in favor of the industry that evidence from 1988–1997 could not be used in trials because of the blanket ban on suing tobacco companies in California in that period.

In 2003, two Supreme Court rulings (*Gore v. BMW* and *Campbell v. State Farm*) recommended that the level of punitive damages that can be awarded should not typically be more than a single-digit multiple of compensatory damage awards. This ruling placed a cap on the financial incentives for speculative claims.

Furthermore, the *Engle* case (2003) was seen as a death knell for the days of multibillion-dollar class-action lawsuits because the punitive award of US$145 billion was thrown out. As a result, over the past decade, the valuation discount between US and non-US tobacco stocks has narrowed significantly.

A lasting legacy of US litigation is that, as **Table 3** shows, the domestic manufacturers have lower credit ratings than non-US tobacco companies with comparable leverage. The structurally weak credit ratings restrict these companies' freedom for balance sheet leverage to fund share repurchases or acquisitions. They also make US domestic tobacco companies more expensive for non-US companies to acquire.

Table 3: Global vs. US Domestic Manufacturers Credit Ratings, March 2014

Companies	Standard & Poor's Rating	LFY Net Debt/EBITDA
Global manufacturers		
JT	AA–	0.3×
PMI	A	1.8
BAT[a]	A–	1.6
IMT[b]	BBB	2.3
US domestic manufacturers		
Altria	BBB	1.4×
IMT[b]	BBB	2.3
Reynolds American	BBB–	1.1
Lorillard	BBB–	1.0
Vector	B	0.9

[a]BAT owns 42% of Reynolds American.

[b]The United States accounts for 4% of revenue.

Note: LFY = last fiscal year.

Source: Based on data from Bloomberg.

Litigation remains an ever-present and evolving risk for the industry around the world. The most notable legal challenges are currently in Canada. The provincial government of British Columbia is seeking to recover tobacco-related health care costs from the industry. In September 2005, the Health Care Costs Recovery Act (British Columbia) was declared constitutional by the Supreme Court of Canada. The act

- allowed British Columbia's government to pursue action on behalf of the people of British Columbia (removing the industry's "remoteness" defense);
- allowed statistical proof to be used as prima facie evidence of damage (bypassing the need to prove causation for each individual case); and
- made the court work under the assumption that a "harm" had been committed.

As shown in **Table 4**, third-party reimbursement lawsuits were also filed by the governments of New Brunswick (2008), Ontario (2009), Newfoundland and Labrador (2011), Alberta (2012), Saskatchewan (2012), Manitoba (2012), Quebec (2012), and Prince Edward Island (2012). Quebec is seeking C$60 billion, and Ontario is after C$50 billion. The governments of Nova Scotia and Nunavut also plan to take action.

Table 4: Third-Party Reimbursement Claims by Canadian Provincial and Territorial Jurisdiction

Year Lawsuit Filed	Jurisdiction	Damages Sought	Notes
2001	British Columbia	Unspecified	The lawsuit was filed against Imperial Tobacco Canada; JTI-Macdonald; Rothmans, Benson & Hedges; and the Canadian Tobacco Manufacturers' Council, as well as R.J. Reynolds. Subsequent lawsuits from other provinces have similar defendants. The courts have dismissed an attempt by the foreign parent companies to be removed as defendants.
2008	New Brunswick	Unspecified	The courts have dismissed an attempt by the tobacco industry to challenge the no-win, no-fee arrangement that the New Brunswick government had with its lawyers. The courts have also dismissed an attempt by the foreign parent companies to be removed as defendants. In January 2012, the New Brunswick Court of Queen's Bench dismissed an attempt by the tobacco industry to name as third-party defendants some tobacco manufacturers that are located on First Nations reserves and that supply contraband.

(Continued)

Table 4: Third-Party Reimbursement Claims by Canadian Provincial and Territorial Jurisdiction (Continued)

Year Lawsuit Filed	Jurisdiction	Damages Sought	Notes
2009	Ontario	C$50 billion	In January 2012, a motion by foreign parent companies to be removed as defendants was dismissed by the Ontario Superior Court. This motion is under appeal with the Ontario Court of Appeal. The tobacco industry is also pursuing as third-party defendants other tobacco firms located on First Nations reserves and that supply contraband.
2011	Newfoundland and Labrador	Unspecified	Lawsuit filed in February 2011. As part of the case, the foreign parent companies have brought a motion to attempt to be removed as defendants.
2012	Manitoba	Unspecified	Lawsuit filed in May 2012.
2012	Saskatchewan	Unspecified	Lawsuit filed in June 2012.
2012	Alberta	C$10 billion	Lawsuit filed in June 2012.
2012	Quebec	C$60 billion	Lawsuit filed in June 2012. A constitutional challenge to Quebec's legislation facilitating the lawsuit commenced in 2009 and has yet to be determined.
2012	Prince Edward Island	Unspecified	Lawsuit filed in September 2012.
Pending	Nova Scotia		In June 2011, the Nova Scotia government announced its intention to file a lawsuit against the tobacco industry and to join forces with the Manitoba government in this pursuit by retaining the same lawyers.
Pending	Nunavut		On 5 August 2011, the Nunavut Justice Minister stated that the territory intended to file a lawsuit.

Source: Based on data from the Ontario Tobacco Research Unit.

In addition to the health care recoupment claims, class actions are ongoing in Canada, notably the *Blais* and *Létourneau* suits in Quebec. They were filed in 1998 and certified in 2005 on behalf of a significant number of Quebecers. The plaintiffs are seeking damages of C$27 billion from Imperial Tobacco (a subsidiary of BAT), JTI-Macdonald (Japan Tobacco), and Rothmans, Benson & Hedges (PMI) as a result of addiction to tobacco products and smoking-related illnesses.

Outside North America, lawsuits have been filed in at least 35 countries, including Australia, Nigeria, and Finland. They include individual claims, class-action suits, and health care reimbursement lawsuits by governments. **Table 5** provides information on some examples.

Table 5: Selection of Legal Cases outside North America

Jurisdiction	Notes
Australia	The Court of Appeal ruled that smokers' actions are not suitable for class-action treatment and held that personal injury actions are more appropriately brought by named individuals.
Chile	In its only decision on tobacco product liability to date, the Civil Court of Santiago rejected claims brought by a plaintiff in relation to an individual smoking and health claim.
Finland	The District Court of Helsinki rejected three individual smoking and health claims by relying, in part, on an earlier judgment by the Supreme Court that rejected a similar smoking and health claim. Two of the claims are on appeal.
Germany	Seven legal aid petitions were refused because of insufficient legal merit to the claims.
Israel	A decision by the Supreme Court regarding the fundamental legality of a long-running health care costs reimbursement case is awaited.
Italy	The Italian Court of Cassation ruled that the meaning of the descriptor "light" was not actionable in itself in more than 4,000 "light" cases brought by Italian plaintiffs. The cases involved individuals alleging that they were misled into thinking that cigarettes labeled "light" were less harmful than regular cigarettes.
Nigeria	Medical health care recoupment claims have been filed by the Nigerian federal government and the governments of a number of Nigerian states, each seeking costs allegedly incurred in treating smoking-related illnesses. The cases are in their preliminary stages.
Russia	A claim in relation to misleading "light" packaging brought by the Russian Ministry of Health was rejected, and the decision upheld on appeal.
Spain	Civil courts dismissed lawsuits brought by the provincial government of Andalucia and by regional laryngeal cancer associations on jurisdictional grounds for failure to include the Spanish government as a necessary party. The provincial government of Andalucia has since brought a new action before the Court for Contentious-Administrative Proceedings.
Uganda	Class actions were dismissed with court costs ordered against the plaintiffs.

Source: Based on company reports.

COMPETITIVE ANALYSIS

The late 1980s heralded significant change in the tobacco industry with the privatization of state-owned cigarette companies in many of the world's largest markets. They include Japan (1987), East Germany (1990), and during the 1990s, 10 of the 15 countries in the former Soviet Union. The privatizations were part of broad reforms to transform those economies by promoting efficiency and economic growth.

Globalization of the industry followed with rapid expansion, particularly in the newly liberalized Eastern Europe. Progress in emerging markets was halted, however, by the 1997–98 Asian financial crisis, which included currency devaluations and led to an economic slowdown across Eastern Europe.

Around the same time, following a long run of tobacco company successes in lawsuits, the tide of litigation turned against US tobacco manufacturers with the coming of the MSA. The legal defeats had high symbolic value because they motivated other plaintiffs with similar cases.

Faced with a threat to its existence, the industry responded by spinning off US assets to "ring fence" US litigation liabilities. It also spun off nontobacco assets and embarked on sector consolidation. The result was that the share of volume (excluding China) controlled by the Big Four global manufacturers rose from more than 50% in 2000 to 75% in 2012. Imperial Tobacco's acquisition of Altadis (2008) and Japan Tobacco's purchase of Gallaher (2006), the final major deals of this period, reduced the number of global manufacturers from six to four players. **Table 6** shows the mergers and acquisitions (M&As) of the period. The concentration of volumes in a small number of global brands generated significant economies of scale for the Top Four.

Table 6: Major Tobacco Mergers and Acquisitions since 1998

Year	Target	Acquirer	Market	Price (US$ billions)	EV/Sales	EV/EBITDA
2010	Fortune Tobacco	PMI	Philippines	Merger	na	na
2009	Bentoel	BAT	Indonesia	0.5	1×	14×
2008	UST	Altria	US	11.7	6×	12×
2008	Rothmans	PMI	Canada	2.0	na	9×
2008	Skandinavisk Tobakskompagni	BAT	Scandinavia/Poland	4.1	6×	15×

(Continued)

Table 6: Major Tobacco Mergers and Acquisitions since 1998 (Continued)

Year	Target	Acquirer	Market	Price (US$ billions)	EV/Sales	EV/EBITDA
2008	Tekel	BAT	Turkey	1.7	3×	11×
2007	John Middleton	Altria	US	2.2	6×	12×
2007	Altadis	IMT	Western Europe	17.4	1×	13×
2007	Common-wealth Brands	IMT	US	1.9	6×	11×
2007	Lakson Tobacco	PMI	Pakistan	0.7	4×	15×
2006	Gallaher	JT	Global	18.8	4×	13×
2006	Conwood	Reynolds American	US	3.5	8×	na
2005	Hanjaya Mandala Sampoerna	PMI	Indonesia	5.2	3×	14×
2004	Brown & Williamson	RJ Reynolds	US	Merger	na	na
2003	ETI	BAT	Italy	2.7	4×	12×
2003	RTM	Altadis	Morocco	2.0	6×	18×
2002	Reemtsma	IMT	Global	5.8	2×	8×
2001	Austria Tabak	Gallaher	Austria	1.8	2×	8×
2000	Massalin Particulares	PMI	Argentina	0.7	2×	6×
1999	Seita	Tabacalera	France	3.3	2×	10×
1999	Imasco	BAT	Canada	7.4	5×	11×
1999	Rothmans	BAT	Canada	7.5	1×	4×
1999	RJR International	JT	Global	8.0	3×	17×
1999	DEVN	IMT	Global	1.1	4×	10×
1998	Cigarrera La Mod-erna	BAT	Mexico	1.7	2×	na

Note: na = not available.

Source: Based on company data.

Although ever-tightening regulation has dented cigarette consumption in developed markets, it has also raised barriers to entry. For instance, advertising restrictions in many markets make establishing a new brand expensive and time-consuming. Few tobacco markets contain any generic competition. As a result, the industry is dominated by large players with strong consumer brand loyalty. Almost 80% of cigarettes are sold through convenience stores and independent shops, rather than through multiple retailers that can leverage their buying power.

In the face of stagnant or declining cigarette volumes, the industry has been forced to rely on pricing power to sustain its profits and earnings growth. **Figure 17** shows the general pattern of loss in volume and growth in prices. The low price elasticity of demand reflects the habit-forming nature of nicotine.

Figure 17: Average Pack Price Growth by Region, 2007–12

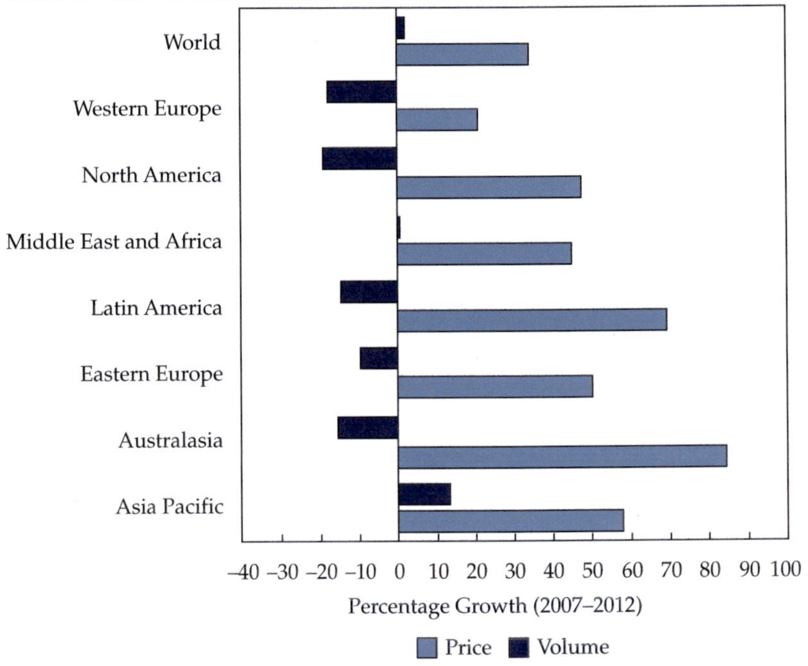

Source: Based on data from Euromonitor.

Figure 18 shows the composition of the price of a typical premium cigarette in several countries. In most countries, manufacturers capture a relatively small share of the money spent by smokers. Thus, when excise tax increases are passed through to consumers, they are frequently accompanied by manufacturer price increases. The market leader controls the profit pool (i.e., profit structure) in each country by dictating the level of manufacturer price increases for all other brands, except for some deep-discount categories.

Figure 18: Distribution of Value of a Premium Cigarette in Selected Markets

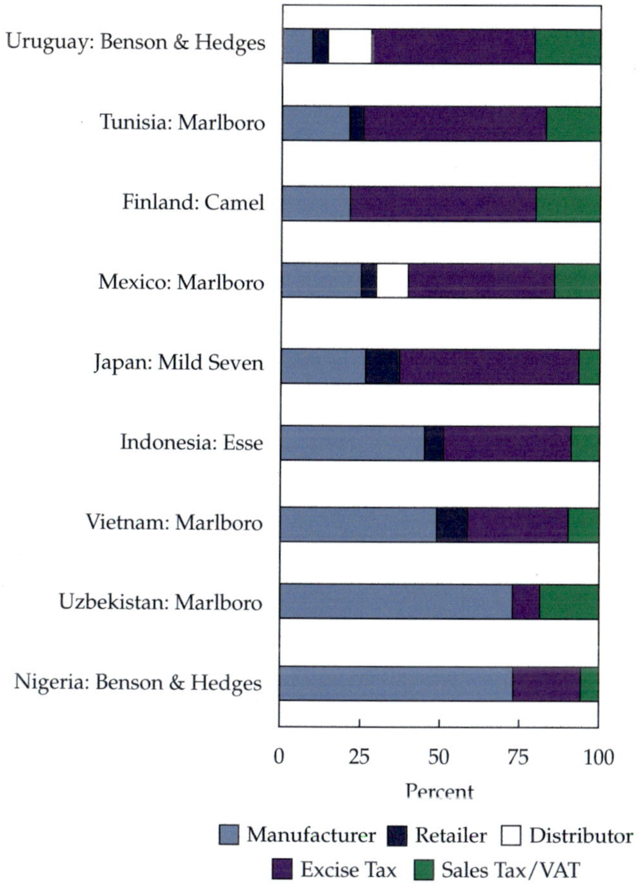

Source: Based on data from *The Tobacco Atlas*.

Nobody really knows how much pricing headroom remains for the industry, especially in developed markets. At some point in the future, tobacco manufacturers will likely face an affordability barrier at which point regular price increases will no longer stick and profits will shrink.

Price competition between manufacturers is frowned on by governments keen to deter new (young) smokers. Price wars have broken out sporadically, however, between premium and discount industry players. An infamous example is "Marlboro Friday," which was 2 April 1993, when Philip Morris announced a 20% price cut to Marlboro cigarettes to fight back against generic competitors. The company's stock price fell by 26% following the announcement, wiping out about US$10 billion from its market capitalization in a single day. The broad market index also fell by 2% on the same day, with notable stock price declines for other branded consumer product companies, such as Coca-Cola and RJR Nabisco.

Less dramatic price wars in the tobacco industry have occurred since then in Germany (2001), the United States (2002), and Spain (2006). In the absence of sustainable volume growth, the industry's profitability remains vulnerable to price-driven competition. Furthermore, a dramatic and wholesale downshift in product mix, from smokers trading down to lower-priced segments (or the illicit trade), will be value destroying for the industry.

This situation has typically occurred in emerging markets when smokers face a sudden and sharp deterioration in disposable income because of the government's economic mismanagement. Historical examples include Southeast Asia (1997), Russia (1998), and Argentina (2002). Manufacturers manage this risk by diversifying their product portfolios to include lower-priced brands for price-sensitive customers. **Figure 19** shows the price segments for developed and emerging economies as of 2012.

Figure 19: Industry Price Segment Mix, 2012

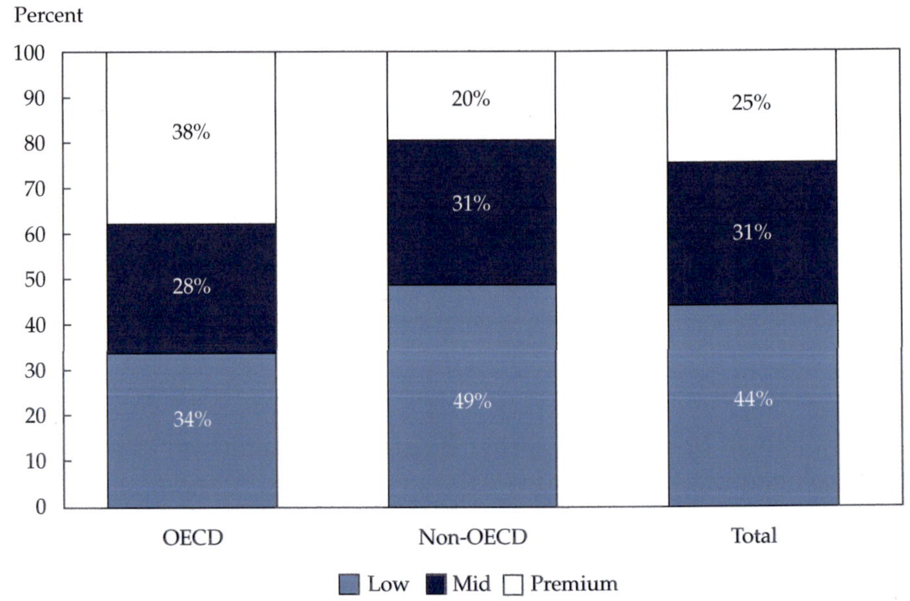

Note: Figure excludes China, the United States, and duty-free data.

Source: Based on company reports.

FINANCIAL STATEMENT ANALYSIS

Despite falling per capita consumption in developed markets, population growth and rising disposable incomes are key top-down drivers of cigarette volumes. The majority of smokers start in their teens, so young adults are the main source of replacement smokers. A company's share of volume of both the young adult market and the older smoker market are, therefore, important metrics to track.

Consumer disposable income is a function of GDP growth, unemployment, and wage inflation. As evident in emerging markets, increasing affluence and affordability increase disposable income and thus drive cigarette consumption. Beyond the level of income seen in developed countries, however, smokers become more risk averse and focus on extending life expectancy.

Because of structural declines in developed-market volumes, changes in tobacco product mix and pricing are strong predictors of relative earnings growth. The reason is that movements in the share of volume by price segment determine how the profits are distributed. The market leader controls the profit pool in each country. And because of advertising restrictions, market share can be difficult to regain once lost. Unusual swings in market share should thus be critically examined.

Bottom-up drivers of sales growth are product innovation and marketing. Because mass market advertising is banned in many countries, manufacturers use innovation to build brand equity and to improve their product mix and profits. The level of new product development should, therefore, be monitored. The main methods of marketing for gaining share are point-of-sale advertisements, promotional allowances paid to retailers for product placements, such promotions as "buy one, get one free," and price discounts.

Operating profit in the tobacco industry typically grows faster than sales. The reason is that price increases boost operating profits disproportionately when variable costs, linked to falling volumes, decline. But the impact depends on the tax structure of a particular country. In general, tobacco manufacturers are able to achieve significant price leverage in countries that levy a greater proportion of the overall excise tax in the form of specific excise (linked to volume) as opposed to ad valorem excise (linked to retail selling price). In the absence of sustainable volume growth, however, price deflation from aggressive competition or trading down can be damaging to profitability.

Tobacco leaf and other direct raw materials account for more than 35% of the industry's total costs, as depicted in **Figure 20**. These costs are primarily US dollar or euro based. As a result, adverse currency movements in emerging markets can have both translational and transactional impacts on the cost of sales and can weaken gross margins.

Figure 20: Industry Cost Breakdown Estimate

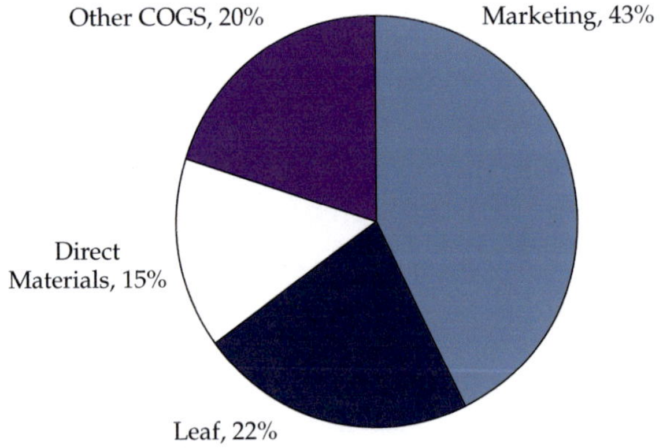

Source: Based on company reports.

Compared with other industries, for tobacco manufacturers, conservative debt levels are a practical necessity as a result of the litigious environment they operate in. The industry is a prodigious cash generator because lack of volume growth limits capital investment needs. The main uses of cash flow are dividends, share repurchases, and acquisitions.

Dividend payments are typically 60%–70% of free cash flow, which makes the industry appealing to income-seeking investors. Share repurchases are also popular among companies in the industry. For instance, in 2008–2012, Philip Morris spent a total of US$27.9 billion on share repurchases. This total was significantly greater than the cumulative dividend of US$24.0 billion paid out during the same period. Share repurchases tend to be irregular; their timing and size depend on balance sheet leverage, acquisition opportunities, and the credit cycle.

Since the last major M&A flurry in 2006–2008, industry consolidation opportunities have been limited to small, "bolt-on" deals (those that provide, for example, cost savings). This approach could change if the Chinese market becomes open to foreign companies. In the long run, China National Tobacco Corporation (CNTC) could also embark on consolidation to become a multinational. CNTC is overseen by China's State Tobacco Monopoly Administration. It manufactures more than 900 cigarette brands, predominantly for China's 350 million smokers. In 2012, fewer than 2% of its cigarettes were exported to other countries. But CNTC is increasing efforts to sell its heritage brands—such as Red Golden Dragon, Dubliss, and Harmony—internationally.

VALUATION

The tobacco industry is part of the global consumer staples sector. Tobacco stocks are traditionally viewed as "defensive" investments because, as a result of regular price increases, they generate relatively reliable earnings growth that is independent of the short-term vagaries in the global economy.

The competitive landscape is also fairly predictable, and the large companies have broad geographical diversification, limiting their risks from local issues. Moreover, the industry has a reputation for shareholder-friendly measures, such as strong dividend growth, share repurchases, and value-enhancing M&As.

Various methods are used to value tobacco stocks, but the most popular one is the P/E multiple because of its simplicity and because tobacco companies convert a high proportion of their earnings into cash.

During the dot-com bubble in the late 1990s, tobacco stocks were viewed as dull, "old economy" investments. Their share prices traded at a significant discount to the broad market. Since then, as **Figure 21** shows, sector P/E multiples have improved as a result of the industry's consolidation, fewer class-action lawsuits, and strong growth in emerging markets.

Figure 21: Historical P/E of Global Tobacco Sector Relative to MSCI World Index, 1999–2013

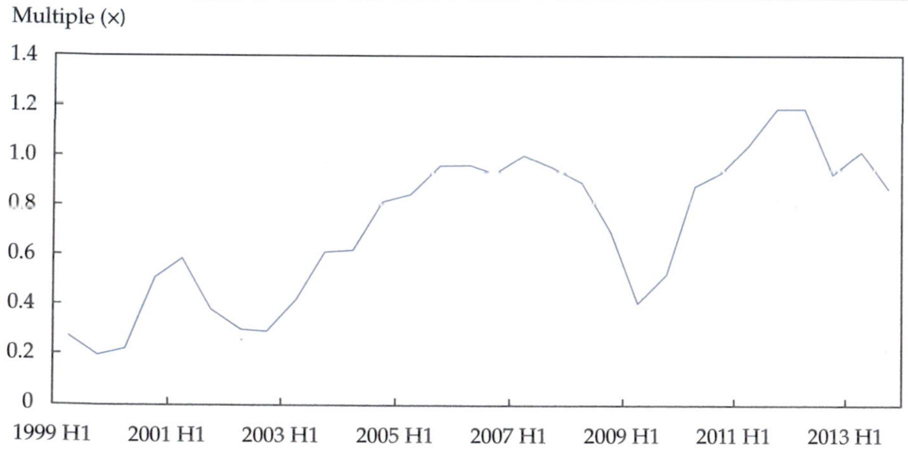

Note: Measured semiannually.

Source: Based on data from Bloomberg.

Because of litigation risk, tobacco stocks usually trade at a P/E discount, however, to other consumer staple stocks with similar growth rates. Also, small tobacco manufacturers in emerging markets typically have takeover premiums in their P/E multiples to reflect the prospect of industry consolidation. Among the large developed-market players, stocks that have exposure to rapidly growing emerging markets and that also control the profit pools trade on higher P/E multiples.

Various scenarios can be modelled with a discounted cash flow (DCF) measure to reflect the industry's structural decline. For instance, some analysts have an explicit forecast period for future cash flows when price increases continue to offset volume growth until, at an inflection point, smoking is banned altogether. No terminal value is assigned beyond that point. Other analysts model an explicit period of cash flow growth because of price increases, followed by a constant rate of cash flow decline in perpetuity with a hard core of smokers keeping the industry afloat. A rosy scenario, usually voiced by industry executives, foresees manufacturers attracting a younger generation of smokers with reduced-risk, regulatory-approved nicotine products that contain no tobacco or smoke toxicants.

To overcome input estimation errors in the wide range of DCF outcomes, some analysts favor a reverse-DCF analysis. Rather than trying to estimate growth into the future, this method takes the current share price and backs out what is currently implied. The resulting implied growth estimate is then compared with historical growth rates to assess differences in the long-term growth prospects priced into the shares of tobacco companies as well as the likelihood of a company meeting or exceeding market expectations.

In the present low-interest-rate environment, tobacco stocks are also viewed as "bond proxies" (i.e., high-yielding stocks perceived to offer "safe" dividends, so they resemble bonds in terms of providing low-risk income). The dividend yields on tobacco stocks are thus compared with government bond yields to assess their relative value. A normalization of bond yields, against a backdrop of a stronger global economy and the US Federal Reserve tapering off economic stimulus support, could lower the P/E multiples on developed-market tobacco stocks.

INDUSTRY RESOURCES

TOBACCO MERCHANTS ASSOCIATION

The premier source of information on the global tobacco industry. Paid subscription is required.

www.tma.org

THE TOBACCO ATLAS

Published by the World Lung Foundation and the American Cancer Society, this free resource offers a large volume of data and information on the global tobacco industry. The fourth edition of the printed publication was released in March 2012, but regular updates are available online.

www.tobaccoatlas.org

THE TAX BURDEN ON TOBACCO

Published since 1949, this publication is the main source for US tobacco tax information. It has key information on federal, state, and local taxes from all 50 US states and the District of Columbia.

www.taxadmin.org/fta/tobacco/papers/tax_burden_2012.pdf

WORLD HEALTH ORGANIZATION

This source provides regulatory health updates from the global body representing 177 countries.

www.who.int/tobacco/en

EUROPEAN COMMISSION

This source provides regulatory updates affecting the 28 EU member countries.

www.ec.europa.eu/health/tobacco/portal/index_en.htm

TOBACCO CONTROL LAWS

This database provides global tobacco industry regulation and litigation.

www.tobaccocontrollaws.org

TRADE JOURNALS

Tobacco International
www.tobaccointernational.com

Tobacco Journal International
www.tobaccojournal.com

Tobacco Reporter
www.tobaccoreporter.com

Tobacco Asia
www.tobaccoasia.com

World Tobacco
www.worldtobacco.co.uk

SCIENTIFIC PAPERS

The peer-reviewed journal *Tobacco Control* is a source of scientific information.
www.tobaccocontrol.bmj.com
See the University of California, San Francisco, library.
www.library.ucsf.edu/tobacco

LEADING CONFERENCES

Tobacco Merchants Association Annual Meeting and Conference

Held since 1915, this perennial event brings together equity analysts, industry executives, and regulators to discuss the state of the global tobacco industry.
www.tma.org

Global Tobacco Networking Forum

Dubbed the "Davos of Tobacco," after the World Economic Forum in Davos, Switzerland, this international gathering regularly features equity analysts, tobacco executives, and public health advocates.
www.tobaccoreporter.com/gtnf-2013

Consumer Analyst Group of New York

The Consumer Analyst Group of New York is an international association of investors and analysts that organizes one-on-one meetings, small group gatherings, and field trips for the investment community with executives from the tobacco, fast-moving consumer goods, luxury goods, and food retail industries. Paid membership is open to all eligible professionals from the investment community and from the covered industries. The EU has its own subgroup, the Consumer Analyst Group of Europe.

www.consumeranalystgroupny.com
www.cag.eu.com

Made in United States
Troutdale, OR
11/03/2026

56844895R00031